Just the Facts

ADHD

Philippa Pigache

Heinemann Library
Chicago, Illinois

Customer Service 888-454-2279
Visit our website at www.heinemannlibrary.com

Produced by Monkey Puzzle Media
Designed by Jane Hawkins
Originated by Ambassador Litho Ltd.
Consultant: Andrea Bilbow, ADDISS
Printed and bound in China by South China Printing Company

08 07 06 05
10 9 8 7 6 5 4 3 2

Library of Congress Cataloging-in-Publication Data
A copy of the cataloging-in-publication data for this title is on file with the Library of Congress.
ADHD/ Philippa Pigache
ISBN 1-4034-5142-7

Acknowledgments
The publishers would like to thank the following for permission to reproduce photographs:
ADD Consults p. 20; AKG-Images pp. 8, 9; Alamy pp. 14 (David Young-Wolff), 17 (Jackson Smith), 25 (David
Young-Wolff), 26 (David Freeman/Fog Stock), 36 (Margaret Mitchell), 42–43 (Plain Picture/S. Kuttig); Corbis pp.
4–5 (Jon Feingersh), 6 (Norbert Schaefer), 13 (Patrik Giardino), 19 left (Franco Vogt), 21 (LWA-Dann Tardif), 35
(Francisco Villaflor), 37 (ER Productions), 44–45 (Lynda Richardson), 46 (LWA-Dann Tardif), 49 (Bettmann), 51
(Mug Shots); Mark Henley p. 11; MPM Images p. 31; Photofusion p. 7 (D. Christells); Rex Features pp. 1 (SIPA),
19 right (Affinity), 23 (Saukkomaa/LHT), 29 (SIPA); Science Photo Library pp. 24 (BSIP V&L), 27 (Dept. of Nuclear
Medicine, Charing Cross Hospital), 28 (Alfred Pasieka), 30 (Jim Varney), 32 (James King-Holmes), 41 (Tracey
Dominey), 40 (R. Maisonneuve/ Publiphoto Diffusion), 47 (Hattie Young); Topham Picturepoint p. 38
(A Thurlby/Syracuse Newspapers/ Image Works).

Cover photograph: main image: Rex Features/SIPA; second image Corbis/Franco Vogt.

The case studies in this book are based on factual information. In some case studies and elsewhere in this book,
names or other personal information may have been changed or omitted in order to protect the privacy of the
individuals concerned.

Contents

Introducing ADHD

ADHD stands for Attention Deficit Hyperactivity Disorder. Yes, it's a mouthful. This is because it is an illness defined by symptoms: in this case, things people do. People with ADHD don't have obvious symptoms such as blotchy skin, a bad cough, or a runny nose. They look just like other people. They are, in fact, just like other people in nearly every way. But a small difference in how their brains work causes them to behave in a way that can make their lives and those of their families and friends very difficult.

Not all people with ADHD have the same symptoms, but all of them have one or more of the following problems:
• they have difficulty paying attention
• they cannot focus on just one thing at a time
• they find it almost impossible to sit still
• they do things without considering the consequences
• they lose things, forget things, and can't keep track of what they're supposed to do.

ADHD is a condition that chiefly affects children. It affects adults too, but the damage it does to children's lives can be much greater because it also affects their families, friends, classmates, and teachers. It can prevent children from making friends, get them into trouble, make them unable to finish their homework, break up their families, and turn their classrooms into chaos.

As doctors get better at recognizing the signs and symptoms of the condition, more people—adults as well as children—are being diagnosed with ADHD, and more people are receiving treatment. Experts believe that at least three children in every hundred between the ages of four and fourteen, and possibly many more, may have ADHD.

Not all of them are seen by doctors of course. In countries where there are so few doctors that even life-threatening diseases go untreated, no one keeps a record of who may have ADHD. But research that has been carried out in many countries leads us to believe that the same proportion of children have ADHD whether they are in Hong Kong or Honolulu, Australia or Africa.

Mental illness

It's not difficult to recognize that a person is ill if there are clear, physical signs of illness. If they have a pain, or an infection that produces a fever, or they eat something that makes them feel sick and throw up, others feel sympathetic and want to help. But if something goes wrong in a person's brain, the control-center of the body, they are not so obviously ill.

Nevertheless, a small blip in the way the brain functions can cause mental illness that can make a person seem unhappy, strange, or difficult to deal with. Instead of offering sympathy, people may say things like: "Pull yourself together," "You've got no self-discipline," "His parents can't cope," or "She's just going through a stage." They do not realize that he or she may not be able to control their behavior.

Children with ADHD may find it impossible to concentrate long enough for even simple board games.

"He was charging around the house waving this plastic machine-gun like a loony. He knocked all the plants off the window sill and broke them."

(The older sister of an ADHD sufferer)

Who's ill? Who's normal?

A broken arm attracts sympathy, but children with ADHD can drive others crazy.

Today, scientists and doctors are beginning to understand the causes of ADHD and other illnesses that affect how people behave. We have progressed from the days when all mentally ill people were locked up, but there is still much prejudice regarding illnesses that affect the brain. It's hard not to view the difficult behavior of a child with ADHD simply as naughtiness or laziness.

Children with ADHD sometimes act like normal children, but because they are ill they cannot stop themselves. For example, all young children have a lot of energy. But a child with ADHD might run around around like a race car in overdrive. Children with ADHD are hyperactive compared with other children of the same age. All children find it difficult to constantly pay attention to a teacher, or to listen carefully to the instructions for playing a new game, but a child with ADHD finds it almost impossible. Children often act without thinking—they can sometimes be impulsive. But a child with ADHD may run across a busy street even when his or her mother has explained a thousand times that it is dangerous. This behavior is no more the child's fault than having a sore tooth or a broken arm, but it doesn't make those around them want to help. It often makes others furious.

The History of ADHD

There are very few new diseases, but there are many new names for old ones. The more that doctors and scientists understand what causes healthy as well as unhealthy behavior, the more detailed and accurate they become in describing and naming old conditions or illnesses.

In 400 B.C.E., the Greek physician Hippocrates described people who had "quickened responses to sensory experience, but were also less tenacious because the soul moves on quickly to the next impulse." If you change "quickened" to "impulsive," put "less able to concentrate" for "less tenacious," and use "hyperactive" instead of the "soul moving on quickly," you have the characteristics that make up a modern diagnosis of ADHD.

In 1902 a British children's doctor, George Still, noticed that a group of his patients—mostly boys—exhibited a pattern of difficult behavior that had started before age eight.

The Greek physician Hippocrates, who lived 2,500 years ago, described people who suffered from something very similar to ADHD.

These children were inattentive, hyperactive, and resisted discipline. In the language of his time, Still said they showed "lack of moral control"—we might say they were "naughty." Still's patients probably had ADHD plus another disorder called oppositional defiant disorder or conduct disorder, a condition that often accompanies ADHD (see page 12). Still believed that the cause of this behavior was inborn, not due to bad parenting or bad environment. This is what doctors continue to believe today.

From 1918 to 1919 there was a massive influenza (flu) epidemic. Flu can cause inflammation of the brain, and many people who survived the illness developed ADHD-like symptoms. This led to the mistaken idea that ADHD is caused by brain damage.

In 1937, by a happy accident, Charles Bradley, a U.S. doctor, used a stimulant drug called amphetamine to treat children who were in a hospital due to their disturbed behavior. Their behavior improved—they calmed down and became more able to concentrate. This was unexpected, because stimulants normally make people livelier, more talkative, and a bit careless. It took another twenty years for specially developed stimulants to become the first-line treatment for ADHD and for doctors to discover why they work in this way.

Over the next 50 years there was much debate about whether hyperactivity or inattention was more important, and about whether there were two different types of ADHD. Then, in 1987, the American Medical Association agreed on the name Attention Deficit Hyperactivity Disorder.

Some experts believe that the British leader Winston Churchill may have had ADHD as a child.

9

Who Is Affected?

With few exceptions, estimates of how many people have a disease or disorder are informed guesswork. In the case of ADHD, all we can say with confidence is that the same percentage of children develop the illness wherever they live, whether they are rich or poor, and whatever culture they come from. However, in countries with less-developed health and education systems these children are less likely to receive treatment for the condition. In the United States, the number of prescriptions written by doctors for the drugs that treat ADHD increased by five times in the 1990s. This is partly because doctors are getting better at recognizing the symptoms, so more children are now diagnosed, and also because sufferers stay on the drugs into adult life.

Most ADHD statistics come from the United States, but there have also been significant studies carried out in other places, including Australia, Brazil, Canada, Chile, China, Germany, India, Indonesia, Israel, Nigeria, Puerto Rico, Thailand, and the United Kingdom.

How many are affected?

Estimates of the number of ADHD sufferers have been increasing. An estimated four or five children in every one hundred between four and fourteen years old have ADHD (conservative estimates suggest three in every one hundred). Estimates vary widely, partly because the list of symptoms and signs used to diagnose the illness is not the same in every country. Estimates also vary because what doctors consider normal behavior varies. For example, what Japanese and U.S. doctors consider to be normal levels of hyperactivity in children, Chinese and Indonesian doctors rate as exceptional levels.

A child has the same chance of developing ADHD no matter what country or culture he or she comes from.

Boys and girls

More boys are diagnosed with ADHD than girls—many more. Again the exact figures vary, but at least three times as many boys as girls are diagnosed with the disorder, and possibly six times as many. Some experts think this is partly because it is more difficult to identify ADHD in girls because they are generally less hyperactive.

How many adults have ADHD?

The few studies that have followed child sufferers into adult life find that as many as three quarters still have symptoms as adults. Some symptoms, such as hyperactivity, become less severe with age, and those who have had treatment learn strategies and take medication. However, the condition cannot be cured altogether.

Symptoms and Behaviors

People with ADHD can have personalities that might be distracted and daydreamy or wild and stubborn. This is because the four main behaviors that mark the condition—inattention, distractibility, hyperactivity, and impulsiveness—don't always show up to an equal degree. Often either the first two or the second two traits are dominant. Some people have both sets of symptoms, and all children with ADHD have problems with finishing homework, keeping their rooms clean, and getting along with other people.

As many as two-thirds of children with ADHD have other disorders that add to their problems. A third to a half may have oppositional defiant disorder (also known as conduct disorder). Basically this means they are not only inattentive and/or hyperactive, but they are also excessively uncooperative and get angry easily—what we might call hot tempered or cranky (although people with these conditions cannot help it). Up to a quarter may also be anxious or depressed, and up to a third may have general problems with learning: with reading, writing, and even with simple physical skills such as hitting a ball or riding a bike.

It can be difficult to recognize a child with ADHD. Individual symptoms that make up their condition are seen in perfectly normal children. But someone with ADHD has a wide range of symptoms and the condition is a problem that cannot be overcome without help. Parents should try to remember this before using some of the phrases discussed over the next few pages.

The Story of Fidgety Philip

The lines below come from a poem called "The Story of Fidgety Philip." The poem was written more than 150 years ago by a German doctor, Heinrich Hoffmann, who worked in what was then called a lunatic asylum. Perhaps he had met some hyperactive children, because his poem seems to describe the behavior of a child with ADHD.

"But fidgety Phil,
He won't sit still;
He wriggles,
And giggles,
And then I declare,
Swung backwards and forwards,
And tilts up his chair,
Just like any rocking horse;
'Philip! I am getting cross!'"

One condition, many names

ADHD in its lifetime has been called many different names: disorder, deficit, condition, syndrome. This reflects doctors' uncertainty about ADHD more than 100 years after it was first described. In the past ADHD has been called:

- Hyperactive Impulse Disorder
- Developmental Hyperactivity
- Minimal Brain Dysfunction
- Moral Control Deficit

- Hyperactive Child Syndrome
- Hyperkinetic Syndrome
- Minimal Brain Damage Syndrome
- Organic Drivenness

Many normal children show some of the symptoms of ADHD, but for sufferers the symptoms are more severe.

Inattentiveness and distractibility

"Everything I tell him goes in one ear and out the other." Many ADHD sufferers cannot keep their attention focused for a moment, so you never know if they have heard what you said or will do what you asked. However, ADHD sufferers are not consistently inattentive. Sometimes they are with you, and sometimes they are on cloud nine. Some sufferers are distracted by their own thoughts; they are often bright, but sit quietly in class and learn little.

"He goes to his room to get ready for school and half an hour later he has one sock on and is looking out of the window."

(Jane, the mother of an ADHD sufferer)

One hyperactive child can create chaos in a classroom.

Impulsiveness

"He's a nightmare on his bike; he has no sense of the danger." When children act impulsively, they act before they think. No amount of reasoning does any good. They know what they are supposed to do, but ADHD sufferers are not in control of their instinctive impulses. Impulsive behavior can be a particular problem because it makes children do things that are dangerous, such as climbing on roofs or waving sharp knives around. In class they interrupt and talk out of turn.

Hyperactivity

"I could never take him any place where he might break things." ADHD sufferers are often much more active than other children in their age group—some were hyperactive and demanding even when they were babies. On the playground, these children act like wild animals. Back in the classroom they find it impossible to sit still. At home they pace around, making everyone jumpy and exhausted.

Social clumsiness

"She's hurt that her classmates shun her, but she brings it on herself." Though many children with ADHD are sensitive and caring, others have no sense of social rules. They'd love to be popular, but don't understand how to make friends. They often seem pushy or overbearing. Their impulses are so strong they don't notice the effect they are having on other people who think they are just bossy. They often say things or do things that are inappropriate or tactless.

Poor co-ordination

"He's so clumsy; he's the last one picked for any game." Most children with ADHD have problems with fine motor skills—things that require precision, like coloring, writing, and tying shoelaces. Some also have problems with gross motor skills like riding a bike or catching a ball. Some are genuinely clumsy; others appear clumsy because they do things thoughtlessly, on impulse. Some are both.

Disorganization

"He leaves a trail of lost things wherever he goes." Most children are untidy or disorganized to some degree, but a child with ADHD could win trophies for creating chaos: clothes put on backwards, mismatched socks, messages from school that don't get delivered, lost books, and, of course, a bedroom that looks like a tornado hit it.

"She's so disorganized she would eat a Mars Bar and brush her teeth at the same time."

(Gail, the mother of an ADHD sufferer)

Low self-esteem

"She's started to give up without even trying." It is not surprising that, with all their problems, children with ADHD often suffer from low self-esteem. They are usually bright enough to see they are making a mess of things, yet they just can't stop themselves. For a parent, one of the most heartbreaking things is to see how a child suffers from not being able to achieve. They want to win awards and be chosen for the team. All children want to do well and want their parents to be proud of them. Children with ADHD sometimes seem doomed to failure.

Boundless but undirected energy is one of the many symptoms of ADHD.

Living with ADHD

First the bad news...

People with ADHD may feel confused, stupid, overloaded with information, lost, and frustrated. Some sufferers feel that living with ADHD is like "being put into a dark room with things scattered around to trip you. You don't get a flashlight … but everyone else does. You trip around the room, bumping into things, until you finally learn the layout of the room. Then someone moves you to a new room, and the process starts again."

Some people have compared the feeling to watching someone change the channels on the TV every few seconds. You can get a general idea of what is going on, but you miss most of the content. "It's like having a whirlwind in your mind. Everything seems to be blowing around and nothing stays put."

Brothers and sisters

ADHD is a condition that is tough on the child who has it, tough on parents and teachers, and equally tough on brothers and sisters, too. Jenny has a younger brother with ADHD. She says "It's not fair. He is always the center of attention. We have to keep telling him how well he's doing, even when he's being a total idiot. Mom's put a lock on my door because before he was always coming in and breaking things and messing things up."

People with ADHD may feel angry, misunderstood, left out, picked on, and different. Autumn is twelve years old and suffers from ADHD. She says that she never wanted to be diagnosed with ADHD and hates living with the condition. "I don't like to be treated different from anyone else but I am," she says. "My advice to other kids with ADHD is to set goals and have your dream, don't give up, you can do it too!"

And now the good news...

ADHD can be a positive influence, too. People with ADHD can be curious, sensitive, creative, artistic, enthusiastic, athletic, imaginative, loving, funny, and energetic. ADHD sufferers can have as much imagination as anyone else and some produce ideas and pictures that are highly original. The curiosity and boundless energy of ADHD hyperactivity can also be a plus when channeled into constructive activities.

For example, some successful businesspeople and entrepreneurs exhibit the symptoms of ADHD, though they usually have a team of people behind them to compensate for their ADHD limitations.

ADHD sufferers express their creativity in many ways. They may paint, play guitar, produce music, act, or even farm. Communicating in words, though, is often more difficult for them. One exception is Bob Seay of Colorado Springs, Colorado. He started writing at school and is now a successful

❝I was passing a field and was beckoned to photograph it by the inhabitants delicately swaying their petals to the vibration of the wind. They are rather magical ... sad ... beautiful ... mindful, perhaps.❞

"Poppies," by an ADHD sufferer and talented photographer. Someone with ADHD sees things differently, which makes the photographer's description of the scene both original and imaginative.

professional writer. Here, in a passage that is both original and chaotic, he vividly describes some of the many positive aspects of living with ADHD: "See all of your worldly possessions at one time ... because they are all over the floor. (You are) ENTHUSIASTIC; Willing to take a Risk ... constantly surprised by finding clothing you had forgotten about. Able to tie seemingly unrelated ideas together ... In class popularity contests, always voted 'Most Entertaining'; Blows up, but then usually recovers quickly; An unstoppable dynamo of human energy ... Provides job security for writers of Spell Check programs ..."

Nicky's story

Nicky lives in Lincolnshire, United Kingdom. As a young child, he was hyperactive and impulsive, but it wasn't until he went to school that he was diagnosed as having ADHD. He was prescribed stimulant drugs, which helped keep his symptoms under control, but Nicky still had difficulty with his school work. "Things got calmer," says his father, Gerry, "but he was never going to be a university professor." But then Nicky discovered gardening. Plants, soil types, bugs, climate, and cultivation became his doorway to study. At eighteen he got accepted to an agricultural college and hopes to become a gardener.

The untamed energy of a hyperactive child may be channeled into physical and creative achievement.

Jamie's story

Jamie is the youngest of three boys in a family from Sussex, United Kingdom and he always lived in the shadow of his older, brighter brothers. When questions were asked, they were quick to answer, so Jamie never bothered. He wasn't interested in school work, had a problem with reading and writing, and was diagnosed with mild dyslexia. Then when he was about twelve, he was diagnosed with ADHD. Sarah, Jamie's mother, says:

"He was always in trouble both at school and home. He didn't walk from room to room, he jumped, ran, lunged, or rolled on the floor. He would pick things up and hurl them around. Outside, if there was gravel, he'd scoop up handfuls and throw it, with no thought for the consequences. Many windows were broken.

"At school, he lost things, forgot what he was doing and couldn't concentrate for five minutes. He seemed oblivious—in a world of his own. If he was sucked into a favorite TV program, he'd be totally focused, but once it finished, all hell broke loose again.

"Eventually the school's educational psychologist assessed Jamie for ADHD and, with some difficulty, we persuaded him to take Ritalin. I was skeptical of faddish 'designer' drugs and couldn't believe it would work. But it was miraculous. He underwent a total behavior change. He became focused, able to concentrate, walked normally, and he was no longer anti-social. Of course he often forgot to take his pills—a common symptom of ADHD—and I always knew immediately, as his old behavior would resurface.

"For Jamie and all of us, it was a life-saver. He's now 21, has a job he enjoys in construction and is quite the perfectionist— a craftsman in the making."

Jamie says:
"I hated school. I was in the special needs group. I had to be taken out of class for special instruction. It made me feel different. When I took my Ritalin pills, it was embarrassing as I had to go to the school secretary to get them—when I remembered, that is! Ritalin helped me concentrate on what the teacher was saying. I felt calmer, too. For me school was a waste of time. Everything I've learned came from my family, friends, and just living. I just like … to be outside—fishing is terrific and they don't teach that at school!'

Like Jamie, many ADHD sufferers are able to focus briefly on their favorite TV show, but not for long.

What Causes ADHD?

In the past there was little understanding of the way the brain functions. Doctors described mental disorders but were in the dark about what caused them or even what part of the body had gone wrong. Today we are able to study the living brain. First came imaging techniques that showed the structures of the brain. However, this did not help explain what caused ADHD because the brains of those with ADHD have the same structures as normal brains (although recent research suggests that certain parts can be smaller).

Then, in the late 1980s, new ways of viewing the brain were invented that showed what was happening in the brain, and doctors discovered that there were differences in the brains of people with ADHD. In addition, doctors learned more about how illnesses are transmitted, by infection, for example, or inherited from parent to child in the genes. This gave scientists and doctors real insight into the causes and nature of conditions like ADHD that affect the way people feel, think, and behave.

Understanding how certain conditions are handed down from parent to child in genes has increased enormously in recent years.

In the genes

If you look at the families of children with ADHD you usually discover at least one close relative with a similar problem: a father who was always in trouble, a cousin who did poorly in school, an uncle who was always getting into fights. The identical twin of an ADHD sufferer, who comes from the same egg and is made of the same genetic material, will almost always (in 90 percent of cases) share the condition.

This evidence tells us that ADHD is hereditary—it is passed down from parent to child in their genes. Genes are little pieces of information contained in the material of every cell of the body that convey instructions for building each unique individual, making him or her grow and function. Genes do not explain everything about why some people develop an illness and others do not, but they explain a lot.

Environmental factors

Genes make people more or less likely to get certain diseases. Upbringing and surroundings also play a part. For example, a child with ADHD whose parents are very sympathetic, whose school is supportive, and whose family and friends are accepting will do better than one whose parents are irritable or hostile, whose teachers are critical, and who is rejected by those around them.

A supportive environment makes a child more likely to overcome the disadvantages of having ADHD.

25

The normal brain

The human brain is constantly bombarded with the information of everything you see, hear, and feel. The brain also gets messages from inside the body (such as whether you are hungry or whether you are getting a cold) and from your memory (such as who people are). It's like hearing several radio stations overlapping one another.

The brain copes with the potential overload by selecting messages that are important and dumping the rest. To do this, several specialized regions of the brain work together. The command center of the brain tells different parts of the brain what information to deliver and what to filter out. The other parts of the brain carry out these instructions. The brain's command center is known as the frontal lobes (at the front of the head, behind the forehead).

ADHD brains

In the brain of someone with ADHD, information floods in without much filtering. It's like watching a split-screen television with many different scenes pictured all at the same time. Information is recorded, but because there is so much of it the child may respond impulsively without weighing the consequences. Alternatively, he or she may not respond to any of the messages crowding his or her brain. He or she is either impulsive or inattentive—or possibly both.

The brain of an ADHD sufferer endures unfiltered information overload. Sometimes it seems impossible to cope.

Images of the brain

The latest imaging techniques scan the brain to show where there is activity and where there is not. One technique, called SPECT (Single Photon Emission Computed Tomography), measures the blood flow to different parts of the brain. Another technique, PET (Positron Emission Tomography) highlights tiny sugar molecules that have been tagged with a radioactive marker that makes them show up on the scan. The sugar collects in the areas of the brain that are most active and makes them light up. By showing whether the lights are either on or off in significant areas, SPECT and PET scans tell us three things about the brains of people with ADHD:

- the frontal lobes (command center) of the brain are under-active in the ADHD brain compared to a normal brain
- those areas that collect visual and sound information are massively overloaded, suggesting that much unnecessary information is not being filtered out
- when stimulant drugs are taken these differences usually disappear.

SPECT images reveal the location of brain activity by highlighting the blood flow to different areas. This is an image of a normal brain. Some differences seen in SPECT images of the brains of ADHD sufferers can be corrected with drugs.

Neurotransmitters: the brain's messengers

It is an oversimplification to think of the brain as having just one command center and regions that carry out orders. The brain also acts as a whole—a bit like an electronic synthesizer producing a complex musical sound composed of many superimposed tracks.

In the brain, billions of different specialized cells pass messages to one another, like a telephone or a computer. These cells—neurons—communicate with each other by means of chemical messengers called neurotransmitters. Between each brain cell is a small gap called a synapse. When a neuron wants to send a message to a neighbor it releases a neurotransmitter that crosses the synapse and stimulates its neighboring cell. The process sparks a chain reaction between brain cells. More than 50 different types of neurotransmitters have been identified, each one controlling different behaviors or feelings, and active in different regions of the brain.

This image of a section through part of the brain is magnified so that you can see individual cells (neurons), which appear black in the picture. Neurons communicate by releasing various neurotransmitters that stimulate neighboring cells.

Dopamine and noradrenaline

The problems associated with ADHD are caused by an imbalance of the chemical messengers dopamine and noradrenaline in the frontal lobes (the command center) and other important regions of the brain. Noradrenaline is known as norepinephrine in some countries.

Without sufficient dopamine, the child with ADHD cannot pick out the important messages from the flood of information bombarding the brain. The child cannot filter out the irrelevant background noise and focus on what matters. Children with ADHD do not have enough dopamine, though too much dopamine is also a bad thing. People with too much become obsessive: they concentrate too much on one thing—trying to keep their hands clean, for example, even when they're not dirty.

Noradrenaline has a different role. It is the chemical messenger that prompts fight or flight reactions—the instinct of cornered animals to either fight or run away. Noradrenaline gears you up and makes you ready for action. Too little makes people indifferent and bored; too much makes them crave

Too little of the neurotransmitter dopamine in one important area of the brain makes it difficult for ADHD sufferers to focus their attention.

excitement—even when this is inappropriate or even dangerous. When these two important brain chemicals are out of balance someone will have difficulty in paying attention and/or be impulsive and hyperactive.

Dopamine levels

Dopamine levels go up when you are happy and relaxed. In one study, scientists in South Africa found that both dogs and their owners had lower blood pressure and higher dopamine levels after they had been relaxing together for half an hour.

Upbringing and environment

The principal cause of ADHD is an abnormality in brain function that affects behavior. This abnormality is inherited—in other words, it is genetic. However, other factors also need to be considered.

During the last century, experts began to stress the importance of upbringing and environment as factors that help children grow up healthy and happy. Environment, we now know, is every bit as important as the genes inherited from parents. Even conditions like ADHD, which has a known genetic cause, are affected by environment. The behavior of parents, family, and teachers can make things better or worse.

However, it can sometimes be difficult for parents of ADHD sufferers to remain constantly patient. Difficult children—even those who are not ill—can make their parents feel inadequate. And, since ADHD runs in families, a parent may also be struggling with ADHD problems.

Problems at birth

Often, the mother of a child with ADHD had a difficult pregnancy or childbirth. Also, many believe there is a higher risk of a child being born with ADHD if the mother smokes or is exposed to some industrial poisons, like those in weed killers, during pregnancy. The likelihood of ADHD also increases if the baby is seriously undernourished after birth.

Is ADHD caused by something in the diet?

In the 1970s, U.S. allergy specialist Ben Feingold claimed that hyperactivity was caused by naturally occurring preservatives or by additives—chemicals added to food to make it last longer or to give it color. At first, studies seemed to support this idea, but thorough investigation eventually determined that, at most, five in a hundred hyperactive children were negatively affected by diet, and then only slightly. Although there are some children with behavioral problems who are sensitive to certain elements in food—whether added or naturally occurring—experts now believe that many of these cases are not cases of true ADHD. Nevertheless, the parents of many children with ADHD remain convinced that certain foods make the symptoms worse.

The sugar in sweets is known to cause tooth decay. However, the artificial colorants and preservatives in them may sometimes aggravate behavioral problems.

Diagnosing ADHD

Before doctors treat anyone they must be sure what they're treating. This process is called diagnosis. It's also called evaluation. Diagnosis is especially important in ADHD because the behaviors that define the illness—inattention, distractibility, hyperactivity, and impulsiveness—are present to some degree in all children. Doctors must be sure that these behaviors are abnormal for the child's age group. In addition, the mix of symptoms varies from patient to patient, and 50 percent of those with ADHD also suffer from other behavior problems in addition to ADHD. These include conduct disorder or oppositional defiant disorder (being obstructive or defiant), learning difficulties (difficulty reading and writing), or motor disorders (extreme clumsiness and difficulty with physical co-ordination).

"The eye of the experienced beholder is more important than a laboratory-load of tests."

(Dr. Christopher Green and Dr. Kit Chee, *Understanding ADHD*, **1997)**

Specialists make a diagnosis by checking a child's symptoms against standard questionnaires and by testing their behavior.

The diagnosis of ADHD is determined by medical experts, but the first alarm bells are usually sounded by a concerned parent or teacher—often because of underperformance at school. Specialists use a number of techniques to arrive at a diagnosis, but these are usually:

- noting symptoms that show up in the home and school environment
- studying a detailed medical and behavioral history of the child and the family
- testing the child against some objective yardstick—the most widely used are checklists or questionnaires. There are also computer programs that measure how a child performs simple tests and others that analyze brainwaves (electrical activity in various key areas of the brain).

Only after all other problems have been ruled out, and the exact kind of ADHD from which the child suffers has been determined—such as inattentiveness/distractibility with or without hyperactivity and impulsiveness—will the specialist begin to plan a treatment program.

Conditions sometimes confused or combined with ADHD

Experts also attempt to distinguish between children with behavioral difficulties who don't have ADHD, and ADHD sufferers who have other conditions as well. These conditions are: autism, or its milder form, Asperger's syndrome; epilepsy; specific learning disabilities; hearing disability; depression; brain injury; family dysfunction (when the behavior of the whole family is the problem); and of course the normally active child whose parents are at their wits' end.

Treatment Programs

There is currently no cure for ADHD. When a child is diagnosed, his or her family knows that they will all have to live with ADHD for the rest of their lives. But there are ways to overcome the symptoms of the condition.

The best results come from combining more than one treatment in a program that includes the child, the family, and teachers.

Specialists who can help

Various educational and medical specialists can offer help and advice for sufferers of ADHD and their families. These include special education teachers, counselors, educational psychologists, behavioral psychologists, physical therapists, pediatricians (doctors specializing in caring for children), psychotherapists, and child psychiatrists. In an ideal world, children with ADHD would have a team of specialists at their disposal and sophisticated machines to monitor their progress. In reality, it is generally parents and teachers who cope, guided by specialists, books, and support organizations.

Drugs plus behavior modification

In most cases, the medication doctors prescribe makes ADHD more manageable. The most successful drugs come from a family called stimulants. Stimulants enable children with ADHD to focus on what is important, retain what they're told, and hold back that impulse to charge ahead without considering the consequences.

Behavior modification is a term used to describe professional psychologists' formal version of what many parents and teachers do when bringing up children. This involves teaching them useful and rewarding ways to control or change their behavior. For example, they might say "Put your homework in your bag tonight so you won't forget it tomorrow." Children can usually be taught simple ways to change their behavior by a mixture of rules, rewards, and punishment. But because children with ADHD don't think ahead or anticipate either positive or negative outcomes, they require specially designed programs. These use repetition, regularity, and endless patience to give them control.

Achieving change

Children with ADHD can organize their lives using a combination of behavior modification and medication. Treatment programs involve parents, siblings, and teachers as well as the child with ADHD. This is partly because the child will need help in achieving change, and also because parents, siblings, and teachers may have to modify their own behavior toward the child. A disruptive child in the family or classroom often prompts people to react negatively—sharp words, lost tempers, bullying, tears, and fights can easily become a common response to children with ADHD at un-medicated full-throttle.

Children, their families, and their teachers need to work together to overcome the symptoms of ADHD.

Behavior Modification at Home

A basic rule of behavior modification is: "Behavior that is not rewarded disappears. Rewarded, it will persist." The difficulty with children with ADHD is that they can't wait for a reward in the future—they need it immediately. So rewards must be small and be given often. A gold star system of rewards allows a child to earn rewards frequently, but the rewards can also add up to a bigger reward. For example, if a child collects enough stars, then they might get to go bowling.

A system of carefully graduated rewards may help combat an ADHD sufferer's tendency to disorganization.

A regular routine

All children benefit from routine. If they do the same things at the same time every day, eventually they will do them automatically. Routine is absolutely vital for children with ADHD who have problems paying attention to instructions and remembering them.

Laying down and enforcing rules

Parents and teachers need to lay down rules to avoid arguments. If a child asks "Can I watch television?", the response might be "Not until your homework's finished—that's the rule."

But rules need to be enforced, so parents must agree on a penalty and enforce it if that rule is broken, keeping firm, calm, and matter-of-fact.

Making lists

Everyone uses lists to jog the memory. Lists help a child with ADHD to keep his or her room clean, complete homework, and finish all the tasks that, unaided, he or she will probably forget. Lists can also help with particular problems: for example, "Things to do if I feel fidgety" or "Things to do if I'm about to lose my cool."

Knowing the danger signals

Parents of children with ADHD learn to recognize the events that risk aggravating their child's symptoms. These might be parties, late nights, visitors, long car trips, or any change in the daily routine. These events cannot be avoided, but measures can be taken. If the child is on medication, for example, doctors may recommend a slightly higher dose to help overcome these situations.

Long car trips

The backseat of a car is often a battleground on long trips. Special measures are required if one of the passengers has ADHD:

- lay down rules, such as no teasing, and agree on penalties if rules are broken
- plan regular breaks and give regular countdowns to the next break
- make sure each child has his or her own toy
- devise games—winning points or treats for spotting things along the road such as animals, particular models of cars, or road signs
- put a large piece of luggage between the occupants of the back seat to reduce opportunities for poking or provoking.

Behavior Modification at School

Some fortunate pupils with ADHD and their teachers get help and advice from an educational psychologist or special education teacher. Ideally, a child with ADHD would have the undivided attention of his own teacher or be taught in a small group—but this is unlikely in most schools. But even in a class of 30, a teacher who understands the problems associated with ADHD can do much to help.

Wherever possible, teachers try to give children with ADHD one-on-one attention.

Capturing the child's attention

A teacher can use a wide variety of measures to capture the attention of a child with ADHD. These may include sitting the child at the front of class or between two quiet pupils, maintaining eye-contact, using animated gestures, and varying the pace and volume of his or her voice to project enthusiasm and excitement. Keeping things short and snappy and asking the child lots of questions also helps to keep him or her involved in the lesson.

Help with organization and memory

A teacher can help a child with ADHD to be more organized by writing things down, on paper or the chalkboard, and by encouraging the child to make lists. It also helps if the teacher divides what the child must do into manageable parts and suggests a set amount of time for each task. In lessons, the teacher may start with an outline and then go into detail. A teacher may also use mnemonics (tricks to jog the memory) and list key words or figures.

Providing support

By understanding that strict discipline does not work for children with ADHD, teachers can help by being firm but tolerant of the child's lapses. Teachers may also show support by giving specific praise: "That's an interesting subject to write about" rather than "That's a good essay." Teachers can also show their support by keeping an eye out for bullying or teasing incidents, and, above all, by never losing their cool.

Working together

By keeping in touch personally (written notes often get lost!), teachers and parents can ensure that the rules the child lives by are consistent, whether these deal with homework, taking his or her medication, or what he or she must wear and bring to school. By sharing the child's problems and progress, parents and teachers can decide if specialized help—counseling, medical advice, or special education classes—is needed.

Treating ADHD with Drugs

ADHD is a condition that affects the brain. Drugs that affect the brain are called psychotropic, which means mind-changing. Alcohol and the nicotine in cigarettes are psychotropic drugs—they change mood and behavior. The drugs with the longest track record of being successful in treating the symptoms of ADHD come from a family of psychotropic drugs called stimulants. Stimulants usually make people awake and excited. However, as we have seen, they also have the effect of enabling ADHD sufferers to concentrate better and control impulsive behavior. They work well for between 70 and 90 percent of those with the condition.

Other drugs may occasionally be prescribed instead of, or in addition to, stimulants. Anti-depressants (which relieve depression) and some non-stimulant drugs can, in some cases, have a beneficial effect on one or more of the symptoms of ADHD.

Drug companies are trying to find safer, more effective drugs to treat ADHD.

How do stimulants work?

For years doctors did not understand why stimulants had an effect on people with ADHD that is opposite to the effect they have on everyone else. They now know that stimulants affect the levels of the neurotransmitters dopamine and noradrenaline (the chemical messengers through which neurons communicate) in those areas of the brain that sift and select important information for attention and control the urge to take action.

Stimulants work fast, taking effect in 15 to 30 minutes. However, the dose that will be effective has to be determined for each person individually, because the time it takes the drug to affect the neurotransmitters varies. Stimulants stop working after four or five hours, so most children need to take them two or three times a day. Medication is now also available that is released slowly over several hours. This means that children with ADHD do not have to take the medicine in front of their friends at school.

The naming of drugs

Even doctors find it difficult to recognize the names of drugs. The names belong to no real, spoken language, but are invented by the people who develop them. In addition, they have at least two names: the name of their active chemical, and a trade name that varies from country to country. The most common medication for ADHD has the chemical name methylphenidate, but the names you will hear most often are its trade names: Ritalin, Metadate (United States), and Equasym (United Kingdom). The first 12-hour extended release drug has the trade name Concerta. You may also hear the chemical name of an older group of stimulants, the amphetamines or dexamphetamines (trade name Dexadrine).

Ritalin 1

The stimulant family

Some stimulants, such as caffeine, are mild; some, such as Ritalin, are medically useful; others, such as cocaine, are dangerous, and often have a frightening reputation.

Just because the stimulant used to treat ADHD has some disreputable relations does not mean it is equally bad. Although there is a family resemblance, different stimulants vary in their precise chemical composition, and this makes them behave differently in the body. Cocaine is addictive: people who use it develop a need for it, can't do without it, and have to take more and more to get the same effect. Caffeine is extremely mild: it would take gallons of coffee to achieve the effect of more powerful stimulants like methylphenidate and dexamphetamine, which are used to treat ADHD. And stimulants that are used to treat ADHD are not addictive when used at the dose prescribed, nor do they make children more likely to grow up to become addicted to other drugs—quite the opposite. When people with ADHD do not receive treatment, they may then be more likely to try harmful drugs because their lives are often a mess.

Drug treatments give children with ADHD a chance to reveal what they can really do—a bit like glasses for the near-sighted.

"When I take medication I can control my ADHD, my ADHD doesn't control me. It helps me fit in with my school friends and be accepted like everybody else."

(James, an ADHD sufferer)

Side effects

All drugs have some side effects that affect some patients. About ten percent of ADHD patients suffer side effects with the most widely prescribed drugs. Side effects mostly occur at the beginning of treatment before the correct dose has been established. They include loss of appetite, difficulty sleeping, and occasional crying or irritability.

Loss of self-esteem

In most cases, the problems children face become more manageable when they take prescribed stimulants. The problem is that parents and teachers may give the impression that this is all the drug's effect, making the child feel incompetent. In fact, the drug is allowing the child's true level of ability to emerge, and parents should reassure children that this is real, not a product of the drug. People should also remember that taking pills is nothing to be ashamed of—it's like wearing glasses or having braces on your teeth.

Can Modifying the Diet Help?

The ancient physician Hippocrates thought that if you had the symptoms of ADHD you should eat "barley rather than wheat … and fish rather than meat." The idea that illness can be caused and cured by diet is still popular today, even after 2,500 years. The discovery of food allergies and intolerances has encouraged people to look for cures that involve changing the food that sufferers eat.

ADHD is no exception. Throughout the 1970s, the Feingold Diet, devised by U.S. allergy specialist Ben Feingold, was thought to be the answer to hyperactivity. Feingold recommended avoiding not only artificial additives but also naturally occurring preservatives in food.

However there is little evidence that anything in food has an effect on levels of inattention or impulsive behavior in children with ADHD, although in a few cases it may have some effect on levels of hyperactivity. Of course, children with ADHD may also have an allergy. If a parent feels that a particular food is aggravating their child's ADHD symptoms, the child may

Salicylates, which occur naturally in strawberries and oranges, can cause an allergic reaction and occasionally aggravate the symptoms of ADHD.

be put on what is called an exclusion diet. He or she starts by eating a very bland, known-to-be harmless diet, such as water, pear juice, unseasoned meat, and preservative-free bread. If their behavior improves, other foods are added one at a time until the ones causing the problem are clearly identified. A diet is then created that avoids the troublesome foods.

Troublesome foods

The following foods may sometimes aggravate ADHD:

- salicylates: these are found in a range of natural foods—strawberries, oranges, tomatoes, and pineapples—as well as in flavorings, colas, and aspirin
- amines: these are chemicals created when food is broken down by fermentation—found in wine, beer, yeast, cheese, chocolate, fish products, colas, and ripe, mushy fruit (such as bananas and avocados)
- monosodium glutamate (MSG): this chemical is found in wheat and many other grains; it is used to improve flavor, notably in Chinese food
- food additives: these include preservatives, added to make food last longer; and colorings, added to make it look attractive.

Alternative Treatments

Parents are naturally worried about giving their children drugs—especially stimulants, which sometimes have a bad reputation. Many parents prefer the idea of a treatment that is natural, although this may be little more than a word used on the packaging of a product. Some remedies promoted for ADHD certainly do no harm, as long as they are not regarded as a substitute for proven, successful medication.

Today, the Internet provides information about many different alternative cures to prescription medicines. Most of these natural products are still manufactured, but they do not undergo the rigorous research—dose testing and investigation into side effects and their interaction with other drugs—that

prescription drugs must go through before they are allowed on the market.

Talking therapies

A talking therapy is a treatment that involves a patient discussing with a trained therapist what they feel and how to change how they feel or behave. This is often helpful. However, many people with ADHD may not have sufficient control over their behavior to benefit from it unless they first take their stimulants so that they can focus on the discussion. Some talking therapies tried for ADHD are: psychotherapy, cognitive behavior therapy, social skills training (training in socially acceptable behavior or good manners), and counseling (discussion aimed at helping the patient).

Many unusual treatments have been suggested for treating ADHD. One is to swing in a hammock, which certainly does no harm!

Physical therapy

Occupational therapists help children with ADHD who have problems with practical physical skills like writing, playing ball, and tying shoelaces. Like other therapies, this works better when combined with medication.

Parenting skills training

Parenting skills training attempts to help family members cope with the problems of living with a child who has ADHD. Together they have training sessions to learn how to respond constructively.

Bio-feedback

In bio-feedback, patients are wired to a machine that records brainwaves and are shown how to control their brainwaves by evoking certain thoughts and feelings. Children with ADHD may be too impulsive or inattentive to master the technique and they may not benefit from this treatment.

Eye exercises

Slow readers often have their sight tested. There is no evidence that ADHD children are more likely to have eye problems than other children, but eye exercises may be tried.

An occupational therapist helps children cope with the physical problems of ADHD.

More unusual treatments

Some of the unusual things tried for treating ADHD have included: cranial (skull) manipulation and realignment of the neck, skull realignment, tinted contact lenses, and swinging in a hammock. Most of these have not been tested by thorough research.

Adults with ADHD

Many conditions, such as asthma, get less severe with age. This appears to be true of some symptoms of ADHD (including hyperactivity). For many years it was believed that ADHD corrected itself as children got older. Then the doctors treating children noticed that there was often an adult in the family who had recognizably similar problems.

ADHD emerges when children go to school. This is partly because, between the ages of four and eighteen, we expect children to sit at desks and study most of the day. In the past, children were expected to learn the practical, physical skills of their parents—hunting, fishing, farming, and raising animals. It seems possible that the symptoms of ADHD might not have been such a severe handicap for those children as they are for children learning to read, write, and do math. And in hunting, the energy and disregard of danger of someone who is hyperactive might even be an advantage.

These days, adults with ADHD may still find jobs that don't require them to sit still or concentrate on one thing for a long time. Some famous actors show the symptoms of ADHD, as do some athletes. Some people who are hopeless in school, like the former British Prime Minister Winston Churchill, nevertheless have successful careers in later life.

Those who are diagnosed in childhood can choose to continue taking their medication and hopefully will also have learned ways to cope with ADHD behaviors. However, in the United States, 40 percent of boys with untreated ADHD commit a crime by the time they reach sixteen and more than half (of those untreated) have drug or alcohol problems.

No one ever says it will be easy. Adults with ADHD are often haunted by a sense of failure or inadequacy. They may work twice as hard to achieve the same result as a person who does not have ADHD, and become workaholics. They are often not as easy to be with and have problems keeping jobs and partners.

Albert's story

Albert was slow to talk and a very poor student in school. His work was messy, he was easily distracted, and he never paid attention or joined in during class. He seemed to live in a dream. As an adult he never had great success in his personal relationships, but while working in the Swiss patent office he started to publish original scientific papers. He won worldwide fame with his revolutionary theories of relativity, and was awarded the 1921 Nobel Prize for Physics. His name was Albert Einstein!

Many experts believe that Albert Einstein had to overcome the obstacles of ADHD. He was not a success at school, but nevertheless went on to win a Nobel Prize.

ADHD Research and the Future

In science, understanding the precise mechanism of an illness is often followed by improved treatment. Throughout the world there is more research into ADHD than almost any other mental disorder. The chief focus of attention is on the genes that increase the risk of developing ADHD.

Identifying genes

By comparing the genes of people who have ADHD with those of people who are unaffected, scientists have discovered slight variations in some genes that increase the risk of getting ADHD. Two genes affect the behavior of neurons (brain cells) so that they take up too much of the chemical messenger dopamine, causing a shortage in key areas of the brain. This excess of dopamine is blocked by stimulants such as methylphenidate. Genes that affect the balance of other neurotransmitters in the brain are also being investigated. Better understanding will eventually lead to new, improved treatments.

New drugs

A recent breakthrough has been the development of a non-stimulant drug for ADHD that works a bit like methylphenidate by correcting the balance of neurotransmitters in the brain. This new drug has recently been released in the United States and will soon be available in the United Kingdom. It is called atomoxetine (trade name: Strattera) and appears to work as well as methylphenidate with reduced side effects such as loss of appetite and sleeplessness. Nevertheless, it will be many years before the new drug builds up a track record comparable to the old tried and tested ones.

Designing a supportive environment for ADHD

Meanwhile, improvements are being made in other forms of treatment for ADHD. For example, we know that, although upbringing and the environment are not the cause of ADHD, they can make things better or worse. Research shows that a negative environment—one where families or schools are hostile and critical—increases the chance that a child with

ADHD will grow up to be a troubled adolescent and adult. When families are trained not to react with anger and hostility to children with ADHD, the child's symptoms are often reduced.

The future for ADHD sufferers is still uncertain. However, greater understanding provides hope that things will improve. This understanding is already contributing to better and earlier diagnosis, and to improved drugs and treatment options. Ultimately, it may contribute to the development of a cure.

When families are trained to support their children with ADHD, these children have a better chance of growing up to become well-adjusted adults.

Information and Advice

A great deal of information about ADHD is available on the web. General background information as well as detailed information about symptoms and treatments can be obtained from various Internet sources.

Contacts

ADDA

(Attention Deficit Disorder Association)
PO Box 543
Pottstown, PA 19464
Tel: 484-945-2101
Email: mail@add.org
Website: www.add.org
This is a comprehensive site, chiefly for adults but with a special 'Kids' corner' and pages for creative writing and pictures.

CHADD

(Children and Adults with Attention Deficit/Hyperactivity Disorder)
8181 Professional Place
Suite 150, Landover, MD 20785
Tel: 800-233-4050
Email: national@chadd.org
Website: www.chadd.org
This is the main US support organization for children and adults with ADHD. It offers a comprehensive range of material.

addconsults

www.addconsults.com
This site offers access to professional advice, articles about ADHD, news of conferences, and features chat, amazing stories, poems and paintings by children and adults with ADHD.

adhd.com

www.adhd.com
This site is geared to sufferers and families. It gives professional advice, has a chat room and features poems and pictures by ADHD children.

adhd.kids.com

http://adhd.kids.tripod.com
This is an original website for 'misunderstood children who thrive outside the box'—the box being the conventional classroom. It offers a space for talented children with ADHD or related problems to express themselves.

More Books To Read

Beal, Eileen J. *Everything You Need to Know about ADD/ ADHD*. New York: Rosen Publishing Group, 1998.

Dwyer, Kathleen M. *What Do You Mean I have Attention Deficit Disorder?* New York: Walker & Company, 1996.

Peacock, Judith. *ADD and ADHD*. Minnetonka, MN.: Capstone Press, 2000.

Silverstein, Alvin. *Attention Deficit Disorder.* Dancury, CT.: Scholastic Library Publishing, 2001.

Glossary

additive
something added, usually to commercial foods to preserve them or add color

allergy
abnormal reaction to a food or something in the environment

amphetamine
type of stimulant drug

Asperger's syndrome
mild form of autism

autism
brain condition that causes children to be withdrawn and unable to relate normally to other people

behavior modification
treating a problem by teaching new ways of behaving

cognitive behavior therapy
treating a problem by teaching new ways of thinking

conduct disorder (also known as oppositional defiant disorder)
stubborn, obstructive, and disobedient behavior

deficit
shortage of something; disability or illness

dexamphetamine
type of stimulant drug

diagnosis
identification of a disease by known symptoms or objective tests

distracted
having difficulty focusing on one thing

dopamine
chemical messenger in the brain that aids selective attention

dysfunction
abnormality in the way something functions

dyslexia
disorder involving difficulty in learning to read or interpret words, letters, and other symbols

exclusion diet
diet that involves the removal of all risk-prone foods, and the gradual inclusion of foods, one by one, to determine which is causing the allergy or intolerance

frontal lobes
region of the brain at the front of the skull that controls selective attention

genetic
related to genes inherited from parents

hyperactive
more active than normal for the age group; *hyper* is Greek for "extremely"

impulsive
acting without thinking or considering the consequences

inattentive
not paying attention

intolerance
abnormal reaction to a chemical in food or the environment

methylphenidate
stimulant drug used in the treatment of ADHD and other conditions

molecules
building blocks of chemicals

neuron
nerve cell that transmits nerve impulses

neurotransmitters
chemical messengers that carry
information between nerve cells

noradrenaline (also norepinephrine)
chemical messenger that prompts fight or
flight reactions

objective
independent—not favoring either one thing
or another

**oppositional defiant disorder (also
known as conduct disorder)**
stubborn, obstructive, and disobedient
behavior

PET (positron emission tomography)
brain scanning technology that records
activity by detecting where radioactively
tagged sugar molecules cluster

physical therapist
specialist who helps people recover from
an illness

psychotherapy
treatment of a mental disorder by
exploring problems with a therapist rather
than with medication

sensory
relating to the sensations you receive via
your eyes, ears, nose, tongue, and touch

**SPECT (single photon emission
computed tomography)**
brain scanning technology that records
activity by identifying differences in blood
supply to parts of the brain

stimulants
chemicals in drugs or food that stimulate
the brain

synapse
gap between one nerve cell and another
crossed by neurotransmitters

syndrome
group of symptoms that occur together
and enable doctors to identify an illness

tenacious
persistent

Index